The Wealth Effects of OCC Preemption Announcements After the Passage of the Georgia Fair Lending Act

Gary Whalen

OCC Economics Working Paper 2004-4

December 2004

The Wealth Effects of OCC Preemption Announcements After the Passage of the Georgia Fair Lending Act[*]

Gary Whalen

Abstract

Rapid growth in subprime lending over the past decade has led to rising concerns about abusive practices by subprime lenders. By early 2004, those concerns prompted Georgia and more than 30 other states to pass laws designed to eliminate abusive or predatory lending practices by the financial services firms, including those with federal charters, operating within their boundaries. In 2003, the OCC concluded that federal law preempts the provisions of the Georgia Fair Lending Act (GFLA) that would otherwise affect national banks' real estate lending. In early 2004, the OCC adopted a final rule providing that state laws that regulate the terms of credit are preempted.

The OCC has asserted that the growing number of state anti-predatory lending laws impose substantial compliance costs on banks, especially smaller, multistate banking organizations that must spread them over smaller levels of output. If these arguments are correct, preemption should reduce expected costs, increase expected revenue, and boost expected bank profitability, especially for smaller banking firms with multistate operations. Opponents of preemption have argued that material preemption benefits for national banks imply a significant competitive disadvantage for state banks and could induce enough state bank charter conversions to endanger the dual banking system.

In this study, an event study approach is used to obtain empirical evidence on the performance effects of preemption. The sample consists of 43 national bank-dominated and 75 state bank-dominated holding companies observed over the October 2002 – January 2004 time period. Briefly, there is not strong evidence of preemption benefits when all national bank-dominated holding companies are viewed as a single group. The univariate tests of portfolio returns and cross-sectional regression results reveal that preemption benefits are larger for smaller, multistate national bank holding companies than they are for both larger national bank companies and similarly sized peers that operate in a single state. This finding is consistent with the view that state anti-predatory lending laws like the GFLA impose a proportionately greater compliance burden on smaller, multistate companies unable to realize economies of scale, which is reduced by preemption. The evidence does not strongly support the notion that preemption places state banking companies at a significant competitive disadvantage. In fact, the excess returns of smaller state banking companies, which comprise the bulk of the state bank holding company sample, tend to be positive rather than negative and typically do not differ significantly from national bank companies with similar characteristics.

[*]The opinions in this paper are those of the author and do not necessarily reflect those of the Office of the Comptroller of the Currency or the Treasury Department. The author would like to thank Mark Hutson for research assistance, Amy Millen for editorial assistance, and David Nebhut, Karen Solomon, and Helen Lai for their comments.

Please direct any comments to Gary Whalen, Senior Economic Advisor, Office of the Comptroller of the Currency, 250 E St., SW, Washington, DC 20219, gary.whalen@occ.treas.gov or (202) 874-4441.

I. Introduction

Subprime lending has grown rapidly over the past decade. Rising concerns about abusive practices by subprime lenders have been a byproduct of this growth. By early 2004, these concerns prompted Georgia and more than 30 other states to pass laws designed to eliminate abusive or predatory lending practices by the financial services firms, including those with federal charters, operating within their boundaries.

Acting on a request from a national bank, the OCC in 2003 concluded that federal law preempts the provisions of the Georgia Fair Lending Act (GFLA) that would otherwise affect national banks' real estate lending. At this same time, the OCC also proposed a final rule to clarify the types of state laws that are applicable to national banks. In early 2004, the OCC adopted a final rule providing that state laws that regulate the terms of credit are preempted. The main features of state anti-predatory lending statutes are typically provisions that restrict or prohibit certain loan terms.

The benefits and costs of these preemption determinations have been hotly debated. The OCC has asserted that preemption results in economic benefits for national banks and does not harm their customers.[1] The agency's basic argument is as follows. State predatory lending laws are numerous, heterogeneous, and complex. The associated costs, especially compliance costs, imposed on banks are substantial. Increased costs could result in a decline in the amount of certain types of credit supplied or an increase in the price. Higher compliance and related costs are likely to be more burdensome for smaller, multistate banking organizations that must spread them over smaller levels of output. If these arguments are correct, preemption should reduce

---

[1] See Williams (2004).

expected costs, increase expected revenue, and boost expected bank profitability, especially for smaller banking firms with multistate operations.

According to the OCC, the application of state anti-predatory lending laws to national banks is not needed to protect the customers of national banks from abusive lending practices because federal supervision, in conjunction with existing federal laws and regulations, prevent national banks from engaging in predatory lending. In addition, clarification of the applicability of state laws to national banks should remove disincentives to subprime lending and increase the supply of credit to subprime borrowers.

Opponents of preemption dispute the view that predatory lending has been sufficiently checked by current federal law, regulation, and supervision. Some have also argued that material preemption benefits for national banks imply a significant competitive disadvantage for state banks and could induce enough state bank charter conversions to endanger the dual banking system.

Detailed data on regulatory costs are not available, and relatively little time has elapsed since the issuance of the preemption rule. Therefore, an event study approach is used in this paper to obtain empirical evidence on the performance effects of preemption. If preemption does reduce expected compliance and other related costs and raise expected bank profitability, positive abnormal stock returns should be evident at holding companies with national bank affiliates around relevant announcement dates. Larger positive excess returns for smaller, multistate holding companies with national bank affiliates constitute support for the notion that the cost burden of state predatory lending laws falls more heavily on this group. Comparison of the abnormal returns of holding companies that have national bank affiliates to those that do not should provide insight on whether or not preemption is likely to undermine the dual banking system.

Briefly, there is not strong evidence of preemption benefits when all national bank-dominated holding companies are viewed as a single group. The univariate tests of portfolio returns and cross-sectional regression results reveal that preemption benefits are larger for smaller, multistate national bank holding companies than they are for both larger national bank companies and similarly sized peers that operate in a single state. This finding is consistent with the view that state anti-predatory lending laws like the GFLA impose a proportionately greater compliance burden on smaller, multistate companies unable to realize economies of scale, which is reduced by preemption.

The evidence does not strongly support the notion that preemption places state banking companies at a significant competitive disadvantage. In fact, the excess returns of smaller state banking companies, which comprise the bulk of the state bank holding company sample, tend to be positive rather than negative and typically do not differ significantly from national bank companies with similar characteristics.

The remainder of the paper is organized as follows. Section II contains some essential background information on subprime lending, anti-predatory lending laws, and the nature of compliance costs. Section III presents the hypotheses examined in the paper. Information on sample selection and selected characteristics of the sample companies is contained in section IV. A chronology of key preemption events is presented in section V. The methodology is discussed in section VI and the key results are detailed in section VII. A summary and conclusions follow.

II. Background

II.a. Subprime and Predatory Lending

Subprime mortgage loans are generally defined as mortgage loans that are riskier than prime loans. This risk difference is clearly reflected in comparisons of the delinquency and foreclosure rates for the two types of loans.[2] As a result, lenders charge higher rates and fees on subprime loans to compensate for the additional risk. In turn, borrowers who would otherwise be denied loans get access to credit. Because subprime loans are potentially profitable and subprime borrowers typically have fewer alternative sources of credit, the potential exists for abusive or predatory practices by subprime lenders.

The benefits to subprime lenders and borrowers are reflected in the relatively rapid growth of this credit market segment over the past decade. Subprime mortgage lending grew at roughly a 25 percent average annual rate since from 1994 – 2003.[3] In 2003, subprime mortgage loan originations were $332 million, about 9 percent of total originations. This 9 percent share represents a doubling since 1994. While the annual level of subprime originations appears relatively modest, the steady growth in originations over the past decade has resulted in a relatively large amount of existing subprime loans outstanding. By 2000, outstanding subprime loans totaled roughly $240 billion and about 42 percent of these loans were securitized.[4]

---

[2] Gramlich (2004) reports that in 2003, 6.75 percent of subprime mortgage loans were delinquent 30 days, 2.12 percent were delinquent 60 days, 3.98 percent were delinquent 90 days, and 3.38 percent were in foreclosure. The comparable percentages for prime mortgage loans were 2.26 percent, 0.58 percent, 0.64 percent, and 0.48 percent. Laderman (2001) also notes higher prepayment risk as well.
[3] These figures are drawn from Gramlich (2004).
[4] Laderman (2001). The proportion of outstanding subprime mortgage loans that have been securitized is roughly in line with that of prime mortgage loans.

II.b. Subprime Lenders

Despite the growth in subprime credit, the number of commercial banks and other financial firms involved in subprime lending and the extent of their involvement is not clear. Available evidence suggests that relatively few commercial banking organizations originate substantial volumes of subprime loans.[5] For example, the last available listing (2002) of lenders subjectively classified as primarily engaged in subprime lending by HUD consists of 183 companies. Only 5 of the companies on this list are commercial banks. Collectively, these 5 banks made 27 percent of the mortgage loans originated by all 183 companies on the list in 2002. Another 19 of these subprime lenders are bank subsidiaries, with a loan share of only 4.4 percent. Thirty-five firms are financial holding company affiliates with the largest aggregate subprime share of 43.0 percent. There are 11 thrift institutions on the list with a 13.8 percent share. Almost two thirds of the subprime lenders on HUD's list are independent mortgage companies that collectively accounted for 11.8 percent of the mortgage loans made by all subprime lenders in 2002.

Other commercial banks and their mortgage banking subsidiaries undoubtedly originate and hold or sell or securitize subprime loans. Other banks also hold some amount of the substantial volume of subprime assets that have been securitized. But the precise number of these bank and bank subsidiaries and the proportion of their revenue, costs, and profitability linked to subprime loans and securities are unknown.

The extent of bank, bank subsidiary, and affiliate involvement in subprime lending is important since it influences the performance effects of preemption. If banks typically have little

---

[5] The following discussion uses data drawn from Gramlich (2004), table 4.

direct or indirect involvement in subprime lending or investors lack information on the importance of this line of business at individual banks, preemption announcements might have little impact on bank stock prices and so result in minimal excess returns.

II.c. Anti-Predatory Lending Laws

Before the passage of the Georgia Fair Lending Act (GFLA) effective October 1, 2002, and similar laws passed by other states, federal legislation existed that was intended to prevent abusive lending by banks. Congress passed the Home Ownership and Equity Protection Act (HOEPA) in 1994, which was implemented as part of Regulation Z, Truth in Lending.[6] HOEPA defines a "high cost" loan using two alternative thresholds; one based on rates, the other on fees. The law then imposes a number of restrictions on "high cost" loans to ensure that loan customers are not exploited by lenders.

The GFLA and other state anti-predatory lending laws generally have forms similar to HOEPA.[7] But the state laws differ from HOEPA and each other in several important ways. Typically, states broaden the definition of loans subject to legal restrictions, and these definitions can vary across states. For example, the original version of the Georgia law created three different loan definitions relevant for lenders: "home loans," "covered home loans," and "high-cost home loans."[8] The rate and fee thresholds used to define "high-cost home loans" are the same as in HOEPA, but points and fees are defined differently, so the Georgia law results in a different, broader set of high cost loans. The list of restrictions, limits, and prohibitions on

---

[6] For a discussion of HOEPA, see O'Sullivan (2003).
[7] For a more detailed description of the provisions of the original GFLA and other similar state statutes, see Lotstein and Shaw (2002), Disque (2003), and Bond (2002).
[8] The original version of the GFLA was amended in 2003.

various lending practices deemed to be predatory for the different loan definitions also vary across states. The targeted practices include prepayment penalties, balloon payments, negative amortization, equity "stripping," loan "flipping," and others.

Penalties for violations of state laws differ across states as well. The penalties for violation of the GFLA are potentially large. The laws of some states, including Georgia, also include provisions for "assignee liability."[9] Assignee liability means that secondary market participants are subject to the same penalties as loan originators for violations of the state laws. This provision makes it more difficult for banks to insulate themselves from adverse effects related to state predatory lending laws, and so increases the incentive for them to incur compliance costs.

In sum, state anti-predatory lending laws like the GFLA are heterogeneous and complex. Penalties for violations are substantial and generally extend to secondary market participants. These characteristics imply potentially large compliance, legal, and other costs for affected banking companies.

II.d. Compliance Costs

There is relatively little reliable empirical evidence on the cost effects of banking regulations. Most of the available studies focus on the tangible costs of complying with individual federal regulations. Few studies provide estimates of foregone revenues, opportunity costs, or litigation costs associated with regulations. The existing studies are relevant, however,

---

[9] A recent report by Standard & Poor's identifies 34 states as having anti-predatory lending laws as of May 13, 2004. The laws of 20 of these states are deemed to include assignee liability.

7

because the primary impact of the GFLA and similar state laws is likely to be on bank compliance costs.

Much of the existing literature on the cost effects of bank regulation is reviewed in Elliehausen (1998). His analysis of available studies indicates that a significant portion of compliance costs reflect the need for banks to use highly skilled, expensive managers and staff experts (legal, lending, data processing, etc.) to comply with regulatory requirements. Computer hardware and software expenses typically represent another significant percentage of compliance costs. In general, these factor inputs tend to be indivisible and so serve as a potential source of economies of scale in regulatory compliance. He concludes that existing studies do support the existence of economies of scale in compliance, which means that average compliance costs for smaller banks exceed those of larger banks.[10] This finding is consistent with the notion that smaller banking companies might realize more benefits from preemption than larger banking companies.

The studies reviewed by Elliehausen do not investigate the costs of complying with multiple, heterogeneous, related regulations like state anti-predatory lending laws. But it is reasonable to assume that the compliance burden imposed by such laws increases the greater the number of states in which a bank operates, given its size. This implies larger preemption benefits for small multistate banking companies than for similar sized companies operating in a single state.

---

[10] For some recent anecdotal evidence on this point, see Thompson (May 3, 2004).

III. Hypotheses

Event studies assume that expected profitability changes stemming from some announcements show up in the excess stock returns of affected firms as investors react to new information. The main focus of these studies is univariate tests that indicate whether or not the average excess stock returns or cumulative average excess returns of portfolios of affected firms are significantly different from zero.

If the GFLA and similar state laws impose substantial costs on banks, related preemption announcements by the OCC should lower expected costs, and increase the expected profitability of national banks. Higher expected profitability implies positive excess national bank stock returns. But stock returns are available only for holding companies, and holding company returns reflect the expected performance of a collection of bank and nonbank affiliates. It is not atypical for a holding company to own both national and state-chartered bank affiliates, and the proportion of consolidated operations accounted for by each charter type to vary across companies. The background information previously discussed implies that any increase in expected profitability for a given national bank resulting from a preemption announcement is likely to depend on a variety of factors, including its size, the geographic scope of its operations, and its business mix. The implication is that the excess returns for holding companies in response to preemption announcements will vary with the relative importance of the national bank component of the company, and possibly other characteristics as well.

Given this circumstance, the approach taken here is to investigate a series of hypotheses about the effects of preemption using a number of different portfolios of holding companies. The first portfolio is based on the assumption that excess returns related to preemption vary directly with the percentage of consolidated holding company operations represented by national banks. Since preemption removes the restrictions of the state anti-predatory lending statutes for national banks and their subsidiaries, national bank-dominated holding companies – those that are primarily made up of national bank affiliates – are probably most likely to exhibit significant positive excess stock returns on preemption announcement dates. Given this likelihood, the first null hypothesis tested is as follows:

HO_1 : On preemption announcement dates, the average excess stock return of national bank-dominated holding companies is insignificantly different from zero.

Rejection of this hypothesis suggests that state predatory lending laws imply a meaningful compliance cost burden on national banks that is removed by federal preemption. But there are a number of reasons why a broad portfolio of national bank-dominated holding companies might exhibit statistically insignificant announcement day average excess returns or alternatively support might be found for HO_1. One possibility is the "mixed" nature of several of the preemption announcements made by the OCC. For example, several of these announcements provided information not only about the agency's preemption intentions, but also about its supervisory policy for predatory lending by national banks. A second reason for the absence of a significant positive announcement effect is the possibility that either the courts or Congress could successfully block or overturn any OCC preemption decision.[11]

There may be other reasons for muted stock price reactions by national bank-dominated holding companies in response to preemption announcements. Characteristic factors like size, business mix, etc., may be more important determinants of preemption-related excess returns

---

[11] See Heller (April 8, 2004) detailing efforts by U.S. Senators to pass a resolution that would overturn the OCC's preemption decisions. National banks do substantial mortgage lending through operating subsidiaries and the extent to which state laws and state supervision apply to operating subsidiaries are also being determined in a number of court cases. See Heller (May 7, 2004) for one such example.

than the percentage of company operations housed in national banks. Thus only a subset of all national bank-dominated companies might exhibit positive excess returns. Another possibility is that investors lack sufficient information about the subprime lending activities of banks to identify accurately the holding companies most likely to benefit greatly from preemption.

The second portfolio of interest consists of state bank-dominated holding companies – companies dominated by state-chartered bank affiliates. Preemption announcements might have a number of possible impacts on state bank-dominated holding companies. If preemption significantly benefits national banks and implies a competitive disadvantage for state banks that remain bound by the restrictions in state anti-predator laws like the GFLA, negative average excess returns for state bank-dominated holding companies should be observed on preemption announcement dates.

There are a number of other reasons, however, why average excess returns for a portfolio of state bank-dominated companies might not be negative. One reason is, like national bank-dominated companies, excess returns for individual state bank-dominated companies might depend more strongly on factors other than the percentage of company operations represented by state-chartered banks. Another is that companies put at a competitive disadvantage by federal preemption can eliminate any disadvantage quickly and at low cost merely by reorganizing their operations (charter conversion, reorganizing a bank subsidiary) or chartering or buying a national bank. Muted stock price reactions also might occur if investors expect state legislatures to alter their anti-predatory lending laws in response to preemption or market developments (e.g., the actions of rating agencies), easing any cost burden on banks.[12] A related possibility is changes in state laws for state-chartered depositories stemming from the existence of "parity provisions."

---

[12] The GFLA was amended in March, 2003. New Jersey took similar action in 2004. See Bergquist (June 29, 2004).

So to obtain insight on which if any of these arguments are correct, the following two null hypotheses are tested:

HO_2 : On preemption announcement dates, the average excess stock return of state bank-dominated holding companies is insignificantly different from zero.

HO_3 : On preemption announcement dates, the average excess stock return of state bank-dominated holding companies is equal to that of national bank-dominated companies.

Portfolios of companies are also created based on measures of size and geographic scope. Tests of the average excess returns of those sorts of portfolios provide greater insight on the existence of any compliance economies. Previous research has found economies of scale in compliance for individual federal regulations, implying higher average costs for smaller banking companies. The cost burden of state predatory lending laws on smaller multistate institutions is likely to be even greater since companies operating in more states face a greater potential burden from multiple state regulatory requirements. If these arguments are correct, smaller multistate companies may be more likely to benefit significantly from preemption, everything else equal. Accordingly, average excess returns for portfolios of smaller, multistate national bank-dominated companies may exceed those of other companies. Two different hypotheses are used to provide insight on this issue:

HO_4 : On preemption announcement dates, the average excess stock return of smaller, multistate national bank-dominated holding companies is insignificantly different from zero.

HO_5 : On preemption announcement dates, the average excess stock returns of large, small, multistate and small single state companies are the same.

In the study, a subjectively determined $10 billion asset threshold is used to separate large from small holding companies. The group of smaller companies was further partitioned into multistate and single state groups. Multistate companies are defined as holding companies with affiliated bank or thrift offices in more than one state. The multistate determination is relatively crude since it was made on the basis of bank and thrift deposit data drawn from the FDIC's Summary of Deposit (SOD) file for June 30, 2003. Thus this determination does not reflect any interstate lending operations conducted through banks, bank subsidiaries, or holding company nonbank affiliates.

As is typically the case in most event studies, a cross-sectional analysis of the excess returns of individual companies is also conducted to determine if and how excess returns vary with company characteristics. Estimated excess returns for individual companies are regressed against measures of affiliate charter types, size, geographic scope, business mix, and location. This approach may provide greater insight on the most important factors influencing excess returns than are gained from the univariate tests based on the performance of the various broad portfolios of sample companies.

IV. The Sample

The sample is drawn from bank holding companies with total assets of $1 billion or more whose daily stock prices are available on the Bloomberg telerate system over the period from October 1, 2002, through January 24, 2004. Holding companies are deleted if they are owned by a foreign entity, are dominated by a special-purpose bank, if they experienced a material confounding event over the interval of observation, or if stock price data were missing.[13] These deletions resulted in a preliminary sample of 156 companies.

---

[13] All acquisition targets were excluded. Acquiring institutions were excluded if the total assets of the target entity exceeded 10 percent of the pro-forma assets of the combined firm. Four additional firms were excluded because a bank affiliate converted from a state to a national charter over the observation period.

Because the stock price responses of holding companies to preemption announcements may depend on the relative size of their national bank component, the analysis is conducted using portfolios of the sample of companies split into "national bank-dominated" and "state bank-dominated" sub-samples. A number of different subjective decision rules could be used to construct these two groups. Here the most stringent possible rule is used.[14] National bank-dominated companies are defined as those where national bank affiliates make up 100 percent of total bank assets. State bank-dominated companies are those where national bank affiliates account for zero percent of bank assets. This classification rule results in portfolios consisting of 43 national bank-dominated companies and 75 state bank-dominated companies. The identities of these companies are included in the appendix. Table 1 contains mean, median, minimum, and maximum values for selected characteristic variables for each of these two groups.

The descriptive statistics for the holding company size measure, consolidated total assets, reveal that the national bank-dominated holding companies in the sample tend to be somewhat larger than the state bank-dominated companies. Both the mean and median total asset values of the former exceed that of the latter. The relatively low median total asset values indicate that smaller holding companies make up the bulk of the sample.

The mean and median numbers of states in which the companies have banking offices are relatively low for both groups of holding companies. The mean number of states for national bank-dominated companies is less than 4, and roughly 2 for state bank companies.

The data for the number of offices of affiliated federal savings association offices show that a few of the sample holding companies operated this type of depository. This is potentially

---

[14] The analysis was also conducted using alternative bank charter type classification rules. For example, a 75 percent national bank asset share cutoff was used to construct the national bank dominated group. In general, changes in the classification rule did not change the findings in any material way.

relevant because the OTS preempted anti-predatory lending laws for federally chartered thrifts in a number of states, including Georgia, over the period of observation.

The descriptive statistics for the two residential real estate loan variables indicate that national and state bank-dominated companies have similar proportions of both types of loans in their portfolios. The roughly comparable mean and median values of the ratio of home equity loans to total loans at the two groups of companies are of interest because this ratio serves as a relatively crude proxy for the extent of holding company involvement in subprime lending in this study.[15]

Finally, the relatively low mean and median values of the two deposit-based indicators of the location of holding company operations reveal that very few of the sample companies have a significant retail presence in Georgia.

V. A Chronology of Key Events

The GFLA became effective on October 1, 2002. It was not the first state anti-predatory lending law passed, but it was generally viewed as the most stringent such statute in existence at the time.[16] In January 2003, Standard & Poor's stated that it would no longer rate mortgage pools containing loans originated in Georgia because of the assignee liability provisions in the statute. The other major ratings agencies subsequently followed suit. Shortly thereafter, the OTS preempted most of the GFLA for federally chartered thrift institutions.[17]

---

[15] Laderman (2001) reports that more than three quarters of the lending done by institutions identifying themselves as primarily subprime lenders was home equity lending. See also Hu (1999).

[16] It was preceded by the North Carolina law, which was effective in October 1999.

[17] See Office of Thrift Supervision (January 22, 2003).

On February 21, 2003, the OCC announced that it would publish for comment a request that it had received from several affiliated national banks and their operating subsidiaries for an agency order or determination that the GFLA did not apply to national banks or their subsidiaries.[18] In supporting documents released at this time, the OCC emphasized that any decision on the merits of the request would focus only on the Georgia law. On the same day, the OCC also issued two advisory letters to help national banks avoid engaging in abusive or predatory lending practices.[19] One letter addressed issues related to direct lending, while the other dealt with issues related to brokered or purchased loans. In these letters, the agency identified most of the potentially abusive practices proscribed by the GFLA and other similar state laws, and indicated that these practices were likely to trigger supervisory action.

In early March 2003, in response to adverse lender and rating agency reactions to the initial version of the GFLA, the Georgia legislature agreed to amend the statute, altering several of its more onerous provisions. In particular, the "covered loan" definition was deleted and the assignee liability provisions were tempered, but not eliminated. Shortly thereafter, rating agencies indicated that they would resume rating mortgage loan pools that included subprime loans originated in Georgia.[20]

On July 24, 2003, in a speech to the Federalist Society, the Comptroller strongly hinted that the agency would preempt the GFLA shortly.[21] The Comptroller's remarks included a discussion of the OCC's authority to make preemption determinations and supporting Supreme Court decisions. He ended by noting that "in preemption situations, the only relevant issue is

---

[18] For details, see OCC (February 26, 2003).

[19] See OCC Advisory Letters 2003-2 and 2003-3 both issued February 21, 2003.

[20] See Bergquist (March 10, 2003) and National Mortgage News (March 17, 2003). In August 2003, the regulator of state banks in Georgia further ruled that the amended GFLA did not apply to state-chartered Georgia banks.

[21] On the following day, the headline on the story about the speech in the American Banker was "Hawke: Get Set for Preemption of Ga. Loan Law."

whether the state law would impair or interfere with the national bank's exercise of powers granted to it under federal law. If such an impact is found to exist, federal law must prevail...".[22] This statement implied that the OCC would determine that other state anti-predatory lending laws are also preempted in the near future.

The following week, on July 31, the OCC issued an order finding that federal law preempts the GFLA for national banks and national bank subsidiaries operating in that state.[23] Simultaneously, given the large and growing number of similar laws in other states, the OCC issued a notice of proposed rulemaking (NPRM) to amend its regulations to add provisions clarifying the applicability of all state laws to national banks.[24] These proposed provisions identified the types of state laws affecting national bank and bank subsidiary lending operations that are preempted and those that are not.

This NPRM also included an explicit anti-predatory lending standard designed to minimize the likelihood that national banks engage in abusive lending practices.[25] In addition, the NPRM contained a reiteration of the agency's position that national bank lending activities are subject to the provisions of Section 5 of the Federal Trade Commission (FTC) Act, that abusive lending practices may be found to be deceptive and unlawful under Section 5, and that the OCC has the authority to bring enforcement actions against national banks that violate this or other laws that the OCC has jurisdiction to enforce.[26]

Finally, on January 7, 2004, the OCC issued a final rule adopting amendments to its regulations to clarify the applicability of state law to national banks and their subsidiaries and

---

[22] See Hawke (July 24, 2003), p. 9.
[23] For the detailed order see OCC (August 5, 2003), pp. 46264-46281.
[24] The NPRM is detailed in OCC (August 5, 2003), pp. 46119-46132.
[25] Specifically, the proposal would prohibit a national bank from making a loan based primarily on the foreclosure value of the borrower's collateral.
[26] This view was previously stated in the guidance issued in February.

identify the types of state laws that are preempted by federal law and those that are not.[27] The final rule includes state laws that attempt to limit the terms of credit in its listing of preempted statutes. Accordingly, most provisions of state anti-predatory lending laws likely would fall into the preempted category. The final rule also included the proposed anti-predatory lending standard and prohibited national banks from engaging in unfair or deceptive practices within the meaning of Section 5 of the FTC Act.

Selection of the appropriate announcement dates in event studies, especially in the case of legal/regulatory decisions is critical and inherently subjective. Here four dates on which key information on the OCC's position on preemption were chosen for analysis. The four dates are February 21, 2003, July 24, 2003, July 31, 2003, and January 7, 2004. These dates and a brief summary of the information conveyed to the market are detailed in table 2.

Although the OCC explicitly stated in February 2003 that the decisions made with respect to the GFLA were not to be interpreted more broadly, all four of these announcements are viewed as related and sequential in this study. Even the first announcement signaled a broader application of preemption beyond Georgia since state anti-predatory lending laws in other states contained similar restrictions on banks and so raised similar issues. The July 24 speech also hinted at a much broader preemption policy. If the four announcements are related and sequential, it is appropriate to examine the sum of excess returns over all four dates for portfolios of holding companies with operations beyond Georgia for evidence of the effects of preemption.

VI. Methodology

---

[27] The final rule is contained in OCC (January 13, 2004), pp. 1904-1917.

A multivariate regression model (MVRM) is used to estimate excess returns in this study. This approach has been used in a large number of previous empirical analyses of the economic effects of changes in financial regulations.[28] There are a number of advantages associated with using the MVRM. Most notably, this technique permits testing for the effects of multiple, related announcements and remedies statistical problems associated with the clustering of sample firm event dates. These equations are estimated using daily return data over the period from October 1, 2002, through January 23, 2004. This interval begins roughly 90 days before the first event date and ends 10 days after the last event date.

The version of the MVRM used here consists of a set of n equations, one for each company in the sample, where each equation has the following general form:

$$(1) \qquad R_{it} = a_i + b_{1i}R_{mt} + b_{2i}R_{mt-1} + \sum_{j=1}^{k}\gamma_{ij}D_j + e_{it}$$

where:

R_{it} = the daily return for company i on day t

R_{mt} = the daily return for the market index (S&P500 Index) on day t

R_{mt-1} = the daily return on the market index on day t-1

D_j = a dummy variable that takes on a value of 1 on event day j, otherwise = 0

e_{it} = the residual error term for company i on day t

n = the number of companies in the sample

k = the number of event days

This system of n equations is estimated simultaneously using the technique of "seemingly unrelated regressions" (SUR). The SUR method results in correct hypothesis testing despite the

---

[28] See for example Saunders and Smirlock (1987), Millon-Cornett and Tehranian (1989), Billingsley and Lamy (1992), Sundaram, Rangan and Davidson (1992), Bhargava and Fraser (1998), Carow and Heron (1998), Cyree (2000), Johnston and Madura (2000), Carow (2001A), Carow (2001B), Carow and Heron (2002) and Narayanan, Rangan, and Sundaram (2002).

presence of heteroscedasticity and cross-correlation of residuals resulting from a clustering of event dates for the subject firms.

The inclusion of the lagged market return in the specification represents an adjustment for infrequent trading.[29] This adjustment is used because of the considerable number of smaller holding companies in the sample. In the MVRM, each of the four event dates is represented by a single indicator variable D_j, which have a value of 1 on that date, otherwise the variable is set equal to zero. Thus, a one-day window is used for each event date.[30]

The estimated excess return for any single event day j for any company i is $\hat{\gamma}_{ij}$. The formal test to determine whether or not an announcement on a particular event day j has a significant wealth impact for a sample of n companies symbolically is whether or not

$$(\hat{\gamma}_{1j} + \hat{\gamma}_{2j} + ... + \hat{\gamma}_{nj}) = 0.$$

As in other studies using the MVRM, the analysis here focuses on the overall market reaction to a series of sequential related announcements about a particular rule change. Each separate announcement provides new information on possibly changing features of the proposed rule change, as well as the probability that the rule will be adopted. In this case, the market reaction to the rule change for a portfolio of affected firms is the sum of the wealth effects for all of the affected companies over all of the relevant event dates.[31] Symbolically, the test of this joint hypothesis is whether or not $(\hat{\gamma}_{11} + ... + \hat{\gamma}_{1j} + ... + \hat{\gamma}_{n1} + ... + \hat{\gamma}_{nj}) = 0$.

---

[29] This is the approach used in Carow (2001A) and elsewhere. The effect of including an interest rate factor in the equations was also explored. The results were not materially different, possibly because rates were relatively stable over this period. So the results obtained using this specification are not reported.

[30] Event studies use a number of different event windows. Here the relevant event dates are relatively clear and so only a one-day window is employed.

[31] The argument supporting the focus on the sum of returns over all relevant event dates is detailed in Appendix A in Carow and Heron (2002), pp. 482-484.

VII. Empirical Results

VII.a. Univariate Tests

Tables 3 and 4 contain the statistical results from the SUR estimation of the set of equations for the sample of holding companies. Table 3 contains the results for several different portfolios of national bank-dominated companies. Table 4 has similar information for the state bank-dominated companies. Results for a number of different subsamples are also presented in each table. In addition to the results for the portfolio of all sample companies of each charter type, findings are also presented for portfolios of "large" holding companies (total assets of $10 billion or more), "small" companies (total assets less than $10 billion), small multistate companies, and small single state companies.

The information presented for each portfolio is the same. The first column of results for each portfolio shows the mean excess return on each of the four event dates, and the sum of the mean excess returns over all four dates. This last cumulative excess return measure is the focus of the analysis. The next column shows the F statistic for the test of whether or not the mean excess or cumulative mean excess returns are significantly different from zero. The third column shows the number of companies in the portfolio that had positive excess returns on each event date or positive cumulative excess returns over all four days. The fourth column is the z statistic for a sign test that indicates whether or not the proportion of positive returns observed is significantly different from 0.5.[32]

---

[32] Formally, $z = (NPOS - n * 0.5)/(\sqrt{n * 0.25})$ where NPOS is the number of positive returns and n is the sample size.

Turning first to the results for the portfolio of all national bank-dominated holding companies in table 3, cumulative excess returns are 1.62 percent over all four-event dates. The associated F statistic reveals that these returns are not statistically significant from zero and so this test does not lead to a rejection of null hypothesis HO_1. The accompanying sign test does show, however, that the percentage of companies with positive returns is significantly different from 0.5.

Splitting the sample of national bank companies into separate portfolios of large and small firms does show that cumulative returns vary with company size. The mean cumulative excess return is 0.61 percent for large companies versus 1.97 percent for smaller companies. This pattern is consistent with the existence of economies of scale in compliance. But the F statistics indicate that neither of these return measures is significantly different from zero. A formal statistical test also cannot reject that hypothesis that mean cumulative excess returns are the same for the two size groupings.[33] The sign test does indicate that the proportion of positive returns at smaller national bank companies does differ significantly from 0.5.

When the group of small national bank companies is subdivided further into portfolios of small, multistate companies and small, single state companies, mean cumulative excess returns are considerably higher for the former. Mean cumulative excess returns for small, multistate companies are 2.30 percent compared with 1.42 percent for small, single state companies. The F statistic also indicates that returns for the small multistate companies are significantly different from zero, while those of single state companies are not. The sign tests are significant for both groups of companies. A further test also reveals that mean returns differ significantly at small,

---

[33] The F statistic is 1.97.

multistate and small single state companies.[34] These findings provide modest support for the notion that state anti-predatory lending laws impose a greater cost burden on smaller, multistate companies and imply a rejection of hypotheses HO_4 and HO_5.

Cumulative excess returns for the portfolio of all state banking companies are 0.59 percent when totaled over all four-event dates, and do not differ significantly from zero. The sign test is also insignificant. These findings mean that null hypothesis HO_2 cannot be rejected. As is the case, for the national banking companies, cumulative returns do vary with size and geographic scope, and do so in a similar fashion. That is, cumulative returns at smaller state bank companies exceed those of larger state bank companies, and those at smaller, multistate companies, exceed those of smaller, single state companies. Again, this pattern is consistent with the presence of compliance economies. Large state banking companies have cumulative returns of –1.52 percent, the only group of state companies to exhibit negative returns. While large state bank company returns are not significantly different from zero, the accompanying sign test indicates that the proportion of companies with negative returns is significant. Smaller state companies have cumulative excess returns of 0.88 percent when viewed as a single group. When the small company group is split into multistate and single state portfolios, cumulative returns at the former are 1.25 percent, roughly twice the 0.61 percent figure for the latter. None of the cumulative return figures for any of the portfolios of smaller state companies are significantly different from zero, although the sign test is for all small state companies and those operating in multiple states. Statistical tests also do not generally show significant differences

---

[34] The F statistic is 3.39 and is significant at the 10 percent level. When the hypothesis that mean returns are the same at large companies and small, multistate companies, the F statistic is 2.45, which is not significant.

when the cumulative returns of portfolios of similar national and state banking companies are compared.[35] These results imply that hypothesis HO$_3$ should not be rejected.

These results are not generally consistent with the notion that state banking companies are placed at a large competitive disadvantage by federal preemption. In particular, smaller state banking companies, especially those with multistate operations, exhibit positive rather than negative cumulative returns in response to the preemption announcements. There are several possible explanations for the observance of positive returns for state banking companies. The positive returns could reflect investor expectations of subsequent revisions of state anti-predator laws in the wake of federal preemption or the lifting of restrictions as a result of parity provisions. Or they may indicate the relative ease with which state banking companies can realize preemption benefits through a variety of relatively quick, inexpensive organizational changes.

VII. b. Cross-sectional Regressions

Tables 5 and 6 contain the estimation results for several different cross-sectional regressions explaining variation in excess returns across the sample holding companies. The dependent variable is the same in each of these regressions: individual holding company cumulative excess returns over all four event dates. The set of explanatory variables reflect differences in company-specific characteristics that could explain variation in cumulative returns. These include measures of size, geographic scope, the charter types of holding company bank and nonbank affiliates, business mix, and location. All of the equations are estimated to

---

[35] The exception is when large national and state banking company returns are compared. In this case, the associated F statistic is 4.88 and is significant at the 5 percent level.

produce robust or White-corrected standard errors. The summary statistics in the bottom rows of each table show that all of the estimated equations are significant.

The equations in the two tables differ only in the set of indicator variables used to reflect differences in the charter type, size, and geographic scope of the sample holding companies. In the set of equations appearing in table 5, three indicator variables are used to capture differences only in the size and bank charter type of the sample companies. These are the variables NBLT10BIL (set equal to 1 for national bank holding companies with total assets of less than $10 billion), SBGT10BIL (set equal to 1 for state bank holding companies with total assets of $10 billion or more), and SBLT10BIL (set equal to 1 for state bank holding companies with total assets of less than $10 billion). In the set of equations appearing in table 6, two indicator variables are employed in place of each of the smaller size charter type dummies (NBLT10BIL and SBLT10BIL) in an attempt to capture any effects related to differences in the geographic scope of smaller holding companies. The alternative indicator variables in these equations are NBLT10BILMS (set equal to 1 for national bank holding companies with total assets of less than $10 billion that operate in multiple states), NBLT10BILSS (set equal to 1 for national bank holding companies with total assets of less than $10 billion that operate in a single state), SBLT10BILMS (set equal to 1 for state bank holding companies with total assets of less than $10 billion that operate in multiple states), and SBLT10BILSS (set equal to 1 for state bank holding companies with total assets of less than $10 billion that operate in a single state). The indicator for larger state banking companies (STBGT10BIL) is also included in the regressions in table 6. In all of the regressions in both tables, the omitted category of holding companies is national bank-dominated companies with total assets of $10 billion or more.

The first regression in each table shows the estimated equation when only the holding company bank charter type, size, and geographic scope indicator variables are included. The other regressions in each table illustrate the effects of including several additional control variables in the specification.

One of these additional variables is another charter type variable. This variable, TOTFSAOFF, is the total number of offices of any affiliated federal savings associations. This variable is included because the OTS also preempted several state anti-predatory lending laws for federal thrift institutions, including the GFLA, over this period.[36] Several sample holding companies owned such affiliates, and so these announcements might influence their estimated excess returns. If the OTS announcements resulted in positive returns for companies owning federal savings associations, they might exhibit smaller stock price movements in response to similar announcements by the OCC.

Companies more heavily involved in subprime lending should benefit more from federal preemption, everything else equal. As previously noted, home equity lending may be a rough proxy for the scale of a company's involvement in subprime activities. Several ratios and related indicator variables that reveal the extent of holding company involvement in home equity lending are used alternatively as subprime proxies in the estimated regressions. The ratios included home equity loans divided by total loans (HELR), home equity loans + home equity asset backed securities held divided by total loans + total investment securities (HELABSR), and home equity loans + home equity backed securities held + the outstanding balance of home equity loans sold and securitized divided by total loans + total investment securities + total loans sold and securitized (HELABSOBSR).

---

[36] In addition to the Georgia announcement, the OTS also preempted the New York and New Jersey laws over this period. See OTS (January 30, 2003) and OTS (July 23, 2003).

Preliminary analysis found a positive, but possibly nonlinear relationship between these ratios and cumulative excess returns and so indicator variables based on each of these ratios were substituted in the estimated equations. The indicator variable based on a given ratio is set equal to 1 for holding companies where the ratio exceeds a particular sample percentile value. The preliminary analysis revealed that indicator variables based on the 95th percentile values of these ratios had significant coefficients, and so these variables (with variable names HEL95D, HELABS95D, and HELABSOBS95D) are used in the final forms of the reported regressions in the tables.

Given the indirect liability provisions of the GFLA and other state laws, companies that are more heavily involved in secondary market activities might realize more benefits from federal preemption. The ratio of net servicing income divided by total income (NETSERVINCR) is used to attempt to capture the extent of each company's involvement in such activities.

Finally, the benefits resulting from federal preemption might be larger, the greater the percentage of a company's operations in Georgia (and possibly other states with anti-predatory lending laws). Here data derived for the Summary of Deposits report is used to create a crude measure of each company's Georgia business.[37] The variable is bank deposits in national bank affiliate Georgia offices divided by consolidated total deposits (GANBDEPR).[38]

The most interesting results in each table are the signs and statistical significance of the estimated coefficients on the indicator variables reflecting the effects of differences in holding company bank charter type, size, and geographic scope. Since these results are not highly

---

[37] This variable does not necessarily reflect where either the bank or nonbank affiliates of the sample companies make mortgage loans.

[38] A similar variable was created for the state banking companies, but was never significant and so does not appear in the reported regressions.

sensitive to differences in the specification of the estimated equations, the discussion will focus on equation 3 in tables 5 and 6.

The estimated coefficient on NBLT10BIL in equation 3 in table 5 is positive and significant, indicating the cumulative excess returns are higher at smaller national bank holding companies than they are at the large national bank company reference group. The negative significant coefficient on the large state bank holding company dummy (STBGT10BIL) means that cumulative returns are significantly lower for this group than for the reference group. The estimated coefficient on the small state bank holding company group variable (STBLT10BIL) is positive and insignificant, implying that there is no difference between the cumulative returns of such companies and the reference group of large national bank companies. Further tests also reveal significant differences in the estimated coefficients when each possible two-way comparison is made.[39]

The results for equation 3 in table 6 reveal that the preemption announcements primarily benefited smaller, multistate national bank holding companies. The estimated coefficient on the indicator variable for this group (NBGT10BILMS) is positive and significant, indicating significantly higher cumulative excess returns for these companies compared with the reference group of large national bank companies. The coefficient for the small single state national bank holding company group (NBGT10BILSS) also is positive, but is smaller in magnitude and insignificant.

Once again the results indicate that cumulative returns at large state bank holding companies are significantly lower than they are at the reference group of large national bank companies. The estimated coefficient on STBGT10BIL is negative and significant. The

---

[39] The F statistic for the hypothesis test that the coefficient of NBLT10BIL=STBGT10BIL is 17.67, for NBLT10BIL=STBLT10BIL is 3.24, and for STBGT10BIL=STBLT10BIL is 10.94.

estimated coefficients on both smaller state bank holding company groups are positive and insignificant, implying that cumulative returns for these groups are not significantly different from the reference group of larger national bank holding companies.[40] Tests do show that the coefficients on each of the smaller state bank groups differ significantly from that of the large state banking company group.[41] As is the case for the national bank companies, the magnitude of the coefficient on the small, multistate group is larger than that of the small single state group, indicating larger preemption benefits for the former class of companies.[42] Formal tests also show that no significant difference exists when similar groups of smaller national bank and state bank groups are compared with one another.[43] Since most of the state companies in the sample are smaller, these findings imply that state banking companies generally have not been significantly disadvantaged by preemption.

The estimated coefficients on the remaining control variables are in line with *a priori* expectations. Cumulative returns are lower for companies that have federal savings association affiliates. This finding could reflect positive stock price responses to preemption announcements by the OTS. Returns are also higher for companies that are more heavily engaged in servicing activities, suggesting preemption benefits for firms that may have a secondary market involvement in subprime loans. The results also show that companies that are relatively heavily involved in home equity lending, a possible proxy for subprime lending, had higher cumulative excess returns in response to the OCC's preemption announcements. Finally, returns are higher for national banking companies with Georgia operations.

---

[40] The F statistic for the hypothesis test that the coefficient of NBLT10BILMS=STBLT10BILMS is 0.99, which is insignificant.
[41] The two F statistics are 12.70 and 6.92, respectively.
[42] A formal test of the equality of these two coefficients does not reject the null hypothesis.
[43] That is, one cannot reject the null hypothesis that the coefficients on NBLT10BILMS and STBLT10BILMS are equal. The same is true for NBLT10BILSS and STBLT10BILSS.

Taken together, the cross-sectional regression results confirm that preemption benefits vary with holding company size and geographic scope, even when the effects of other important factors influencing excess returns are controlled for. The statistical tests show significant differences in returns when large national bank-dominated companies and smaller, multistate national bank-dominated companies are compared. The same pattern of results is evident for state bank-dominated companies. For both charter types, the highest returns are evident for smaller, multistate companies, followed by smaller single state companies and larger holding companies. These findings imply the rejection of null hypothesis HO_5.

The evidence on differences in returns at national and state bank-dominated companies is somewhat mixed. The cross-sectional results reveal that returns at large state bank-dominated companies are significantly less than that of large national bank-dominated companies. But the statistical tests do not reveal significant differences in returns when smaller state bank-dominated companies are compared with their national bank-dominated peers. Since smaller holding companies comprise the bulk of the state bank-dominated sample, the weight of the evidence is not consistent with the view that federal preemption has put most state banking companies at a significant competitive disadvantage or alternatively that null hypothesis HO_3 should be accepted.

VIII. Summary and Conclusions

In this study, an event study approach is used to investigate the wealth impacts of the OCC's recent real estate-related preemption announcements on national bank-dominated and state bank-dominated holding companies. This approach yields estimates of the expected net economic effects of federal preemption on banks, but this is the only alternative since detailed historical revenue and cost data are not available. The study does not provide any evidence on the impact of preemption on consumer protection. This is an important issue, but it is outside the scope of this paper.

As in all event studies, the findings reflect a considerable number of assumptions made by the researcher. The most notable of these is the inherently subjective choice of the dates on which relevant preemption information reaches the market.

In general, the analysis does not reveal strong evidence of preemption benefits when all national bank-dominated holding companies are treated as a single group. A likely reason for this finding, confirmed by subsequent testing, is that expected preemption benefits vary systematically with holding company characteristics. Univariate tests and cross-sectional regressions do reveal that preemption benefits are larger for smaller, multistate national bank holding companies than they are for both larger national bank companies and similarly sized peers that operate in a single state. A plausible explanation for this finding is that state anti-predatory lending laws like the GFLA impose a proportionately greater compliance burden on smaller, multistate companies unable to realize economies of scale, which is reduced by preemption.

The evidence does not strongly support the notion that preemption places state banking companies at a significant competitive disadvantage. In fact, the excess returns of smaller state banking companies, which comprise the bulk of the state bank holding company sample, tend to be positive rather than negative and typically do not differ significantly from national bank companies with similar characteristics.

Additional research on the impact of preemption is ongoing. In particular, HMDA data will be used to investigate how preemption effects vary with differences in the location of each holding company's mortgage lending operations. HMDA data show where both bank and nonbank affiliates of holding companies originate mortgage loans. In the current study, inferior SOD deposit data are used to determine where each company's operations are located.

References

Bergquist, E. "N.J. to Ease Predator Law, as GA Did in '03," American Banker (June 29, 2004).

Bergquist, E. "Will Georgia 'Fix' Help or Hurt Federal Law's Case." American Banker (March 10, 2003).

Bhargava, R. and D. Fraser. "On the Wealth and Risk Effects of Commercial Bank Expansion into Securities Underwriting: An Analysis of Section 20 Subsidiaries." *Journal of Banking and Finance* 22 (1998).

Billingsley, R. and R. Lamy. "Regional Reciprocal Interstate Banking: The Supreme Court and the Resolution of Uncertainty." *Journal of Banking and Finance* 16 (1992).

Bond, K. "Predatory Lending – A Trap for the Unwary." ABA Bank Compliance (July/August 2002).

Carow, K. and R. Heron. "The Interstate Banking and Branching Efficiency Act of 1994: A Wealth Event for Acquisition Targets." *Journal of Banking and Finance* 22 (1998).

Carow, K. "Citicorp-Travelers Group Merger: Challenging Barriers Between Banking and Insurance." *Journal of Banking and Finance* 25 (2001A).

Carow, K. "The Wealth Effects of Allowing Bank Entry into the Insurance Industry." *Journal of Risk and Insurance* 68, No. 1 (2001B).

Carow, K. and R. Heron. "Capital Market Reactions to the Passage of the Financial Services Modernization Act of 1999." *Quarterly Review of Economics and Finance* 42, No.3 (2002).

Cyree, K. "The Erosion of the Glass-Steagall Act: Winners and Losers in the Banking Industry." *Journal of Economics and Business* 52 (2000).

Disque, H. "The New Jersey Predatory Lending Act." Mortgage Banking (November 2003).

Elliehausen, G. "The Cost of Bank Regulation: A Review of the Evidence." Staff Study 171 Board of Governors of the Federal Reserve System (April 1998).

Gramlich, E. "Subprime Mortgage Lending: Benefits, Costs, and Challenges." Remarks at the Financial Services Roundtable Annual Housing Policy Meeting (May 21, 2004).

Hawke, J. "Remarks Before the Federalist Society." (July 24, 2003).

Heller, M. "OCC Power Over Subsidiaries Tested in Two Court Cases." American Banker (May 7, 2004).

Hu, J. "The Performance of Home Equity Loans." Mortgage Banking (April 1999).

Johnston, J. and J. Madura. "Valuing the Potential Transformation of Banks into Financial Service Conglomerates: Evidence from the Citigroup Merger." *The Financial Review* 35 (2000).

Laderman, E. "Subprime Mortgage Lending and the Capital Markets." FRBSF Economic Letter 2001-38, Federal Reserve Bank of San Francisco (December 28, 2001).

Lotstein, R. "Georgia and Beyond." Mortgage Banking (September 2002).

Millon-Cornett, M. and H. Tehranian. "Stock Market Reactions to the Depository Institutions Deregulation and Monetary Control Act of 1980." *Journal of Banking and Finance* 13 (1989).

Narayanan, R., N. Rangan, and S. Sundaram. "The Welfare Effects of Expanding Banking Organization Opportunities in the Securities Arena." *Quarterly Review of Economics and Finance* 42, No.3 (2002).

O'Sullivan, S. "Predatory Lending: Attempts to Plug the Money Drain." Communities and Banking Federal Reserve Bank of Boston (Spring 2003).

OCC. Notice of Request for Preemption Determination or Order. *Federal Register* 68, No. 38, 26 February 2003. 8959-8964.

OCC, "OCC Issues Guidelines to National Banks to Guard Against Abusive Lending Practices; Invites Comments on Request to Determine that Georgia Law Is Preempted." News Release 2003-08 (February 21, 2003).

OCC, "Guidelines for National Banks to Guard Against Predatory and Abusive Lending Practices." Advisory Letter 2003-2 (February 21, 2003).

OCC, "Avoiding Predatory and Abusive Lending Practices in Brokered and Purchased Loans." Advisory Letter 2003-3 (February 21, 2003).

OCC, Statement of the Comptroller of the Currency John D. Hawke, Jr. Regarding National City Determination and Order (July 31, 2003).

OCC, "OCC Takes Steps to Keep Abusive Practices Out of National Banking System While Ensuring Continued Access to Credit for Low-Income Americans." News Release 2003-59 (July 31, 2003).

OCC. Preemption Determination and Order. *Federal Register* 68, No. 150, 5 August 2003. 46264-46281.

OCC, Bank Activities and Operations; Real Estate Lending and Appraisals. *Federal Register* 68, No. 150, 5 August 2003. 46119-46132.

OCC, "OCC Issues Final Rules on National Bank Preemption and Visitorial Powers; Includes Strong Standard to Keep Predatory Lending Out of National Banks." News Release 2004-3 (January 7, 2004).

OCC. Bank Activities and Operations; Real Estate Lending and Appraisals. *Federal Register* 69, No. 8, 13 January 2004. 1904-1917.

Office of Thrift Supervision. "OTS Says Georgia Law Doesn't Apply to Federal Thrifts." Press Release 03-02 (January 22, 2003).

Saunders, A. and M. Smirlock. "Intra- and Interindustry Effects of Bank Securities Market Activities: The Case of Discount Brokerage." *Journal of Financial and Quantitative Analysis* 22, No. 4 (December 1987).

Standard and Poor's. "Anti-Predatory Lending Law Update." (May 13, 2004).

Sundaram, S., N. Rangan, and W. Davidson. "The Market Valuation Effects of the Financial Institutions Reform, Recovery and Enforcement Act of 1989." *Journal of Banking and Finance* 16 (1992).

Thompson, L. "A Leaner Mercantile: Legal Compliance Big Part of Consolidation." American Banker (May 3, 2004).

Williams, J. Testimony Before the Subcommittee on Oversight and Investigations of the Committee on Financial Services of the U.S. House of Representatives (January 28, 2004).

Appendix

Sample Holding Companies

NB Companies > $10 billion

Banknorth Group
BOK Financial Corporation
City National Corporation
Commerce Bancshares
First Tennessee National
Corporation
Firstmerit Corporation
Huntington Bancshares
Keycorp
TCF Financial Corporation
U.S. Bancorp
Wachovia Corporation

NB Companies < $10 billion, Multistate

Amcore Financial
American National Corporation
City Holding Company
Cobiz, Inc
Community First Bancshares
First Community Bancshares
Integra Bank Corporation
Nara Bancorp
National Penn Bancshares
NBC Capital Corporation
NBT Bancorp
Old National Bancorp
Peoples Bancorp
Riggs National Corporation
State Financial Services
Corporation
Sun Bancorp
UMB Financial Corporation
Valley National Bancorp
Whitney Holding Corporation
Yardville National Bancorp

NB Companies < $10 billion, Single State

Arrow Financial Corporation
Corus Bankshares
Cullen/Frost Bankers
First Indiana Corporation
Harleysville National
Corporation
Omega Financial Corporation

Pennrock Financial Services
Corporation
Seacoast Banking Corporation
of Florida
Southwest Bancorporation of
Texas
Sterling Bancorp
Suffolk Bancorp
Unizan Financial Corporation

STB Companies > $10 Billion

Amsouth Bancorporation
Bank of New York Company
Compass Bancshares
Fifth Third Bancorp
Marshall & Ilsley Corporation
Southtrust Corporation
State Street Corporation
Bancorpsouth
Provident Financial Group

STB Companies < $10 Billion, Multistate

Amercanwest Bancorporation
Banc Corporation
Banner Corporation
Boston Private Financial
Holdings
Capital City Bank Group
Community Banks
Community Trust Bancorp
First Citizens Bancorp of South
Carolina
First Source Corporation
First State Bancorporation
Glacier Bancorp
Gold Banc Corporation
Hudson United Corporation
Irwin Financial Corporation
Itla Capital Corporation
Mainsource Financial Group
Republic Bancorp
Royal Bancshares of
Pennsylvania
S.Y. Bancorp
UCBH Holdings
Umpqua Holdings Corporation
United Community Banks
U.S.B. Holding Company

Washington Trust Bancorp
Wesbanco
West Coast Bancorp
Wilmington Trust Corporation

STB Companies < $10 Billion, Single State

Ameriserv Financial
Bank of Hawaii Corporation
Bank of the Ozarks
Capital Corp of the West
Central Coast Bancorp
Century Bancorp
Chemical Financial Corporation
Columbia Bancorp
Columbia Banking System
CVB Financial Corporation
East West Bancorp
First Charter Corporation
First Mariner Bancorp
First South Bancorp
Frontier Financial Corporation
Iberiabank Corporation
Independent Bank Corporation
Interchange Financial Services
Corporation
Investors Financial Services
Corporation
Lakeland Bancorp
Lakeland Financial Corporation
Macatawa Bank Corporation
Main Street Banks
Mid-State Bancshares
Midwest Banc Holdings
Peoples Holding Company
Privatebancorp
Prosperity Bancshares
Republic Bancshares
S & T Bancorp
Sandy Spring Bancorp
Silicon Valley Bancshares
Southside Bancshares
State Bancorp
Sterling Bancshares
Sun Bancorp
Trico Bancshares
Virginia Financial Group
Westamerica Bancorporation

Table 1

Descriptive Statistics for Sample Holding Companies

Variable	NB-Dominated HCs (N=43)				State Bank-Dominated HCs (N=75)			
	Mean	Median	Min	Max	Mean	Median	Min	Max
Consolidated Total Assets($bil.)	21.683	3.644	1.093	401.032	8.493	2.264	1.022	92.405
Number of States w/ Bank Offices	3.767	2	1	25	2.08	1	1	9
Federal Savings Association Offices	0.0465	0	0	2	0.187	0	0	5
1st Lien 1-4 Family Residential Loans/Total Loans	0.1851	0.1498	0.005	0.407	0.1697	0.1694	0	0.4685
Home Equity Loans/Total Loans	0.0686	0.058	0	0.2418	0.0608	0.0522	0	0.177
Net Servicing Income/Total Income	0.0036	0.0009	-0.0225	0.0256	0.002	0.0002	-0.0115	0.0634
Deposits in National Bank Affiliate Georgia Offices/Total Deposits	0.0024	0	0	0.1017	n.a.	n.a.	n.a.	n.a.
Deposits in State Bank Affiliate Georgia Offices/Total Deposits	n.a.	n.a.	n.a.	n.a.	0.0286	0	0	1

Table 2

Preemption Event Dates

Variable	Date	Announcement
D_1	2/21/2003	OCC announces it is exploring preemption of Georgia Fair Lending Act (GFLA). OCC issues two advisory letters containing guidance on how to avoid abusive lending practices.
D_2	7/24/2003	In a speech to the Federalist Society the Comptroller strongly hints that the GFLA will be preempted.
D_3	7/31/2003	OCC announces it is preempting the GFLA. OCC issues a notice of proposed rulemaking for a regulation that will clarify which state laws apply to national banks and which types of state laws are preempted. The proposed regulation includes an anti-predatory lending standard.
D_4	1/7/2004	OCC issues a final rule that identifies the types of state law that are preempted by federal law and so are not applicable to national banks. The rule includes a new anti-predatory lending standard.

Table 3

Estimated "Day 0" Abnormal Returns by Event Date

HCs w/ 100 Percent National Bank Assets

Event Date	All HCs (N=43)				Assets >= $10 billion (N=11)				Assets < $10 billion (N=32)				Assets < $10 billion, Multistate (N=20)				Assets < $10 billion, Single State (N=12)			
	Mean AR	F stat	# Positive	Z stat	Mean AR	F stat	# Positive	Z stat	Mean AR	F stat	# Positive	Z stat	Mean AR	F stat	# Positive	Z stat	Mean AR	F stat	# Positive	Z stat
2/21/2003	0.0038	0.46	28	1.98**	0.0012	0.03	9	2.11**	0.0046	0.51	19	1.06	0.0054	0.81	12	0.89	0.0034	0.17	7	0.58
7/24/2003	0.0086	2.48	34	3.81***	0.0071	1.15	7	0.90	0.0091	2.02	27	3.89***	0.0099	2.80*	17	3.13***	0.0079	0.88	10	2.31**
7/31/2003	0.0048	0.76	28	1.98**	-0.0004	0.01	5	-0.30	0.0065	1.03	23	2.47**	0.0058	0.98	14	1.79*	0.0077	0.82	9	1.73*
1/7/2004	-0.0009	0.02	23	0.46	-0.0018	0.07	6	0.30	-0.0006	0.01	17	0.35	0.0019	0.11	11	0.45	-0.0048	0.31	6	0.00
Sum	0.0162	2.18	34	3.81***	0.0061	0.21	8	1.51	0.0197	2.33	26	3.54***	0.0230	3.76*	16	2.68***	0.0142	0.71	10	2.31**

***, **, and * indicate significance at the 1, 5 and 10 percent levels, respectively.

Table 4

Estimated "Day 0" Abnormal Returns by Event Date

HCs w/ 100 Percent State Bank Assets

Event Date	All HCs (N=75)				Assets >= $10 billion (N=10)				Assets < $10 billion (N=66)				Assets < $10 billion, Multistate (N=27)				Assets < $10 billion, Single State (N=39)			
	Mean AR	F stat	# Positive	Z stat	Mean AR	F stat	# Positive	Z stat	Mean AR	F stat	# Positive	Z stat	Mean AR	F stat	# Positive	Z stat	Mean AR	F stat	# Positive	Z stat
2/21/2003	0.0007	0.02	37	-0.12	0.0002	0.01	4	-0.63	0.0008	0.02	34	0.25	0.0015	0.05	15	0.58	0.0003	0.01	19	-0.16
7/24/2003	0.0053	0.92	50	2.89***	0.0011	0.03	3	-1.26	0.0059	0.97	47	3.45***	0.0079	1.34	21	2.89***	0.0045	0.59	26	2.08**
7/31/2003	0.0015	0.08	36	-0.35	-0.0063	0.86	2	-1.90*	0.0026	0.19	34	0.25	0.0031	0.21	14	0.19	0.0022	0.14	20	0.16
1/7/2004	-0.0017	0.09	32	-1.27	-0.0102	2.22	1	-2.53**	-0.0005	0.01	31	-0.49	-0.0001	0.01	13	-0.19	-0.0009	0.02	18	-0.48
Sum	0.0059	0.29	44	1.50	-0.0152	1.21	1	-2.53**	0.0088	0.54	43	2.46**	0.0125	0.84	19	2.12**	0.0061	0.28	24	1.44

***, **, and * indicate significance at the 1, 5 and 10 percent levels, respectively.

Table 5

Cross-sectional Regressions

Explanatory Variables	(1) COEFF	t	(2) COEFF	t	(3) COEFF	t	(4) COEFF	t	(5) COEFF	t
NBLT10BIL	0.013578	2.45**	0.014030	2.23**	0.014704	2.33**	0.015874	2.41**	0.014525	2.31**
SBGT10BIL	-0.021275	-2.95***	-0.017570	-2.18**	-0.017906	-2.14**	-0.014352	-1.65*	-0.017257	-2.09**
SBLT10BIL	0.002654	0.55	0.004739	0.84	0.005996	1.04	0.007208	1.17	0.005845	1.02
NETSERVINCR			0.426325	2.47**	0.435157	2.60***	0.433734	2.50**	0.432041	2.51**
TOTFSAOFF			-0.005868	-6.35***	-0.005617	-5.62***	-0.007034	-4.52***	-0.006932	-4.41***
HEL95D					0.018775	2.89***				
HELABS95D							0.013505	1.90*		
HELABSOBS95D									0.013655	2.05**
GANBDEPR			0.179428	3.52***	0.189940	3.57***	0.227034	3.43***	0.211614	3.54***
Constant	0.006099	1.62	0.004065	0.85	0.002184	0.43	0.001349	0.24	0.002695	0.54
F Stat	7.59***		27.48***		18.23***		8.55***		7.77***	
R-squared	0.1314		0.1768		0.2057		0.1902		0.1912	
NOBS	118		118		118		118		118	

***, **, and * indicate significance at the 1, 5 and 10 percent levels, respectively.

Table 6

Cross-sectional Regressions

Explanatory Variables	(1) COEFF	(1) t	(2) COEFF	(2) t	(3) COEFF	(3) t	(4) COEFF	(4) t	(5) COEFF	(5) t
NBLT10BILMS	0.016879	2.50**	0.016862	2.28**	0.017838	2.43**	0.018970	2.49**	0.017553	2.40**
NBLT10BILSS	0.008076	1.24	0.009376	1.33	0.009689	1.39	0.011031	1.55	0.009605	1.39
SBGT10BIL	-0.021275	-2.92***	-0.017399	-2.16**	-0.017735	-2.11**	-0.014016	-1.62	-0.017070	-2.07**
SBLT10BILMS	0.006419	1.07	0.008922	1.36	0.010844	1.60	0.011633	1.65*	0.010176	1.52
SBLT10BILSS	0.000048	0.01	0.001846	0.30	0.002803	0.45	0.004356	0.66	0.002930	0.47
NETSERVINCR			0.366997	2.08**	0.369469	2.20**	0.372367	2.10**	0.370688	2.10**
TOTFSAOFF			-0.006398	-5.72***	-0.006203	-5.07***	-0.007637	-4.46***	-0.007520	-4.30***
HEL95D					0.020166	3.15***				
HELABS95D							0.014185	2.10**		
HELABSOBS95D									0.014258	2.23**
NBGADEPR			0.189841	3.66***	0.202591	3.71***	0.240112	3.60***	0.223670	3.67***
Constant	0.006099	1.61	0.004260	0.90	0.002263	0.45	0.001416	0.26	0.002838	0.58
F Stat	4.77***		14.46***		10.29***		6.23***		5.68***	
R-squared	0.1495		0.1939		0.2270		0.2087		0.2096	
NOBS	118		118		118		118		118	

***, **, and * indicate significance at the 1, 5 and 10 percent levels, respectively.